Also by Dara Wier

In the Still of the Night

Wave Books

SEATTLE & NEW YORK

Dara Wier

IN THE

STILL

OF THE

NIGHT

Published by Wave Books

www.wavepoetry.com

Copyright © 2017 by Dara Wier

Wave Books titles are distributed to the trade by

Consortium Book Sales and Distribution

Phone: 800-283-3572 / SAN 631-760X

Library of Congress Cataloging-in-Publication Data

Names: Wier, Dara, 1949– author.

Title: In the still of the night / Dara Wier.

Description: First edition. | Seattle : Wave Books, 2017.

Identifiers: LCCN 2017011912| ISBN 9781940696560

    (hardcover) | ISBN 9781940696577 (softcover)

Subjects: | BISAC: POETRY / American / General.

Classification: LCC PS3573.I357 A6 2017 | DDC 811/.54—dc23

LC record available at https://lccn.loc.gov/2017011912

Designed and composed by Quemadura

Printed in the United States of America

9 8 7 6 5 4 3 2 1

First Edition

Wave Books 067

Where shall I hide my things? Who is alive?

EMILY DICKINSON

FOR EMILY, FOR GUY, AND FOR JIM

Contents

in the still of the night

when not a thought

chills with not a breeze

anywhere to be found

not a nightbird calling

not a fine light flickering

no crickets, no crickets singing

no far far away train whistles calling

not a rustle

not a shimmer

the way a petal falls

on its own

away from all the others

with no one watching

that's how one human leaves us

In the Still of the Night

An Ant in the Mouth of the Furnace

Sorrow likes itself most when it's

At its best being

A barrier

Impenetrable. An obstacle.

A veil that can't be torn.

When beyond its deckled edges

Sorrow won't let you see.

As if you were a blue blur on paper

Intended to be a child's image of heaven.

And it takes more bearing

Because more of it is always coming.

And it takes up space where space has never been.

Where there is no space.

Where no space has ever been.

And it will not move.

And brings all else to a standstill.

To no longer be in a state of grief is also a state.

To encounter the respite it is

Is to judge

Sometimes one's self

Other times others.

There must be a name somewhere

For what's not there

For what doesn't

By its aggravating presence

Begin to replicate what's gone.

Man overboard.

My life's work.

Black & blue overcoat.

Orange eyes. Bleeding wall.

Ring-tailed neck riverbed blanket.

It's not

As though

After all

Suits every blue circumstance

As if

—What's that—

—What comes after—

After which is

Is no other

After after all

No after other

All as if at

Last all that

That grieving

It is over—

So as to make room for another.

You are doing something

With someone who isn't here.

How many conversations

With who isn't

Able to talk back

Is one human allotted?

Things were only

Like they were

Because we were

Having them together.

Having them without you

Is another thing altogether

Before when

You once were

Here *we* was

A something never failing

We could

Be counted on

We would

Have always been

What we were

No wonder.

That's What the Dead Do

That's what
the dead do.

The ones
who've died,

who have given up
their lives,

who have died for us
so that they say

to us
See here this is

all it means
to be dead—

to be no longer living and
to be both never

and always as never before
and after.

This is all
it means

the dead ones say,
So you die,

and everyone left living
sticks around.

You and everyone
who loves you

and who you love
take some time

to mourn
with speechless desire,

and unspoken awe,
our long faces and

our sideways glances
(as if you might be

somewhere off
to the side),

here we come
with our living

fruit baskets and
soon to wilt white flowers,

good things
intended

to sublimate pain
to substitute one thing for another

& others pay
their respects

& others have their curiosity piqued
& a very few are glad you're gone

though would never dare
say so

& most of all most
can't care at all

and rightly so, everyone
can't be this faced

with this much
that often

& that's what
a death does

beyond doubt
one death says

what every death is,
& what's out of sight

just over the horizon
not so long later,

a year or so
at most,

everyone's up & gone
on to other matters

the kinds of matters
that matter to the living

(your matter's been burned
or by nature's

routine chemistry
mostly dissolved) (but you

knew that)
(you knew all along)

finding reasons
to stay alive

finding work first
for fuel

& then for pleasure
& sex &

maybe love
or what passes

for love
& sex

maybe for adding
another

living human into the mix
for the rest of us

that're left
& other ways

to pass the time.
Once thoughts

about how many of us
there are

involved
in so much

doing and coming
& going & searching

& hunting & gathering
& using up time

& space
& materials.

The Dream

We all know about the classic dream
the one in which you see a door or some other

hithertobefore unknown ingress or egress,
your own private dream annex,

which now is a sign
and to you it signifies

there is something or somewhere
where you are you hadn't been before.

In this classic iconic many times
overtold dream you stumble into a way to wander

into something you'd missed.
Something you hadn't dreamed of before.

So you open the door.
And beyond the door

as the light comes up a little
there is a cave

you'd never known
was there before.

It's as wide and as far
as the eye can see,

with a horizon
as wide and deep as any before.

This cave is huge and it is enormous
and it is gargantuan and it is

immense and it is as expansive
as any space you've ever known.

And just at your feet, right there,
almost as if one could say,

right under your nose, there
is a river, or maybe it's a stream,

it's hard to say
because the space

it's in
is of a proportion you've never known

before
so what might have been a river

in one space is really
just a little stream in another.

It's a river. It's going on forever.
It goes beyond the horizon

that is the cave's far end.
You can follow this river

up and down hill and dale,
up and around and over and after

woods and valley
and mountain range

and hillside and meadow
after another, you

can follow it
for as long as you like,

as long as you're able.
It takes a while.

As you follow it you find
you've time to think.

And what else is there
to think about

but what is the source
of this river.

How if you follow it
you will find its source

and see from where it comes.
So you follow the river

to its source
which turns out to be

at the river's end
a place where up ahead

there's a drive-in movie screen.
A big old nearly beaten down drive-in movie screen.

Just standing there. Doing exactly
what it should be doing, showing a movie.

Only we can't see what
the movie is

because the angle it's taking
is just out of reach

of our field of vision.
There's one car

parked before the drive-in movie screen
and in that one car

there's a bull who looks
pretty much just like a child's Ferdinand,

with brass rings in his nose and all that, and
he's too big for the car

he's squeezed into but there he is,
wedged into the car,

obviously it has to be
a convertible or else

the Ferdinand-like bull
could not really be himself

in it. He is
sitting in it and he bulges out of it.

He is way too big for this
car.

Whatever it is
on the movie screen

is such that
it is causing this bull to weep.

He is weeping buckets.
He can't stop crying.

His tears stream down
his big bull cheeks.

And it is his crying
that's filling up the river

we've been following.
We understand now

it is his tears
filling up the river.

His tears are
the river's source. And we

have found it
at last.

I stay in the dream
when it so happens

still inside
dreaming later,

just a little later,
just a second's dream time later,

I tell my dream lover
about the cave

and the river
and the river's source

and he looks at me
as if I've broken a window

or broken into a lock
meant to stay locked up forever.

And he says,
why do you act like this

and I say because
when I act like this . . .

and I stop here
because with every word

I say
there's confetti

floating from my mouth
and I have to pause

a little to admire how good
confetti can be

as it floats out gently
on waves of air

with a graceful and musically sonorous
rhythm

as it takes turns turning
into first banners,

then clouds,
then puffs

of smoke
from a toy train's chimney,

then warm breath
condensed

in chilly morning's air
and that dream lover

I'd almost forgotten
keeps repeating

why do you act like this,
and I repeat

when I act like this
you call me mask

and because
when I act like this

you think I am you.
More happens

as the dream goes on
but this is probably

plenty enough for now.

The Luxury of Being Depressed

To have the time
and the wherewithal

to be able
to look around

in despair
to be able

to spare
yourself

the lenient necessity
despair craves

to be shocked
by the idleness

alluring
despairing

to descend
to have no desire

to be mired
as in accidie

like a cursed curse
like no other

to be at the mercy of,
of everything vague

and persistent and invisible,
to be without cause,

percentage, repentance,
repute, reasonable doubt

to be smothered
to be spared

love's suffocating
responsibility

to be ashes
drowned

with liquid lava
to be losing one's mind

to be doing so
with pleasure

to give up all else
other than

for instance
rain you see fall

on a pond you know
what ownership is

and how to feel
sad w/o being sad

she said, social
& rubbing shoulders with.

Life understood
backwards,

lived forwards,
lived after the fact

if death
is giving up

love then love is
pretending

there's no end
coming

as in say the lake,
the frozen lake

or how it is
to cut a house in half,

or to leave
most of everything

or everything
behind

some things have to stay backwards
unable

to be reversed and
then

what do
you do

to make sure
something, something

might be possible
in times to come

in times to come

that were once before

if not

resolutely visible.

Free Will

When the baby girl
would not stop crying

I had to wonder
how much pain

unrepeatable,
unbearable

and not to be balmed
can one child suffer?

The blossoming pear trees
invade the city,

and the plums,
and the other

white blossoms
that lead to nowhere

and nothing.
Half the sidewalks

still wet
with what had been

pitiful spring showers.
The other half

not hot enough
to steam.

Some areas hazed
pink with wilting petals.

Some petals stuck
on crosswalks.

Some footprints
evaporating

in the dead center
of spring on this spring

afternoon.
Everything in the background

stays in the background.
As if this might as well be

the beginning of all time.
And this time time

will be kinder to everyone.
Though no one knows

whether this means more
or less of it.

Some people are stuck
with themselves forever.

When we willed eternity
into existence,

we might as well
have damned some of us

to some forever
without end.

What someone says
somewhere for,

for what.
I'm blind to something,

indifferent to something.
An indifferent monster

of oblivion am I,
sometimes.

My carelessness
guarantees

my indifference
will be monumental.

As though
I'd purchased my life

like—
what—

what might
a life be

like other than
what it is.

Like a flattened penny,
like a steamboat.

Like good money
unalike after bad.

My concerns are thin-
strapped and see-through

as any chemise
of cotton and lace.

Sometimes the loud
fake call

of mechanical birds
feels like

a slap in the face.
I've been slapped

in the face once.
But only once.

I've been strangled
but not to the point of lost consciousness.

I've been thrown against a wall.
What difference does it make?

Whether that's a fact
or it might as well have been?

You work backwards.
You take

what we quaintly call
a broken heart.

You take its pieces
in practically undifferentiated parts.

You take your time with them,
turning them over

in your quicksand mind,
the mind with quicksand in it,

so that any little stray
thought

will fall in
and never leave.

If you were the first person
to notice how dangerous

an overindulgence
in material goods is,

something would be
done about it.

If you were the first
to notice

we take advantage
of one another without fail

I'm fairly sure
we'd be living in a different world.

The Front of Me Is Always
on the Dark Side of the Moon

We tend to have so much in common.

How easily our physical properties, skin and blood
and all the soft organs and hard bones, the slippery-
when-wet hair shined by an ointment we produce
as though someone's hairdresser had the deciding
vote when it came time to decide what liquids and
near pastes and other materials our bodies will pro-
duce.

We have rubbery tendons and strangely untangled
ropes of nerves, we share the same calcium-rich
close-to-translucent spade-shaped shields of pro-
tein and keratin on the tips of our fingers and at the
ends of our toes.

For all our differences we have the same adamantly
strong enamel teeth, our eyes are exactly synony-
mous,

muscle & vein & jelly, miraculously joined
to let light articulate shape for our safety and know-
ledge, and more often than anyone is able to ac-
knowledge, for our pleasure, to astonish us, to,
metaphorically anyway, bring us to our knees.

We share a great variety of elements, dry and moist
combinations of oxygen, carbon, hydrogen, nitro-
gen, calcium, phosphorus, potassium, sulfur, so-
dium, chlorine, and magnesium determine what
we are.

Our shared similarities reach back into the slightest
niches—
an idle paleontologist fingering idly around in left-
over fossilized hip bones
directly to the tiny skin tag one's lover habitually
touches just behind one's left ear's cartilaginous
zone.

One evening I watched a man as if in a trance trace his son's earlobe's shape as if it were a mystical track. I saw a woman bite a handful of her own hair.

We share the liquids that fill the chambers that house our progeny.
We neither of us have burning fires within us. We stop short of that.
You might be filled with water and dust and dirt and living and dead creatures, but you do not have fire in you, not anywhere, not at all, none.

My sharing with you every inch of me available to physical description makes us more than brothers or sisters or distant relatives or nearly anything so remotely connected as any DNA samples will reveal. As far as the universe is concerned, we're one and the same, we're identical.

People are always asking one another, if you could be anything in your next life—a great bit of gloriously faux naive subterfuge—what would you be—

I'm sure I'd be a scientist, a chemist of the human elements, someone familiar with our solids and liquids when stable

and in transition. Able to picture our chemistry's parts and pieces and processes and hits and near misses in combination and in dissolution as we become who we are. I would admire and not forget the copper or the silicon or the zinc.

It's hard not to envy any taxonomist's straightforward taking stock, making inventory, inventing classifications, documenting resemblance, noticing

aberration, systematizing, organizing, classifying, sorting, mapping vertical and horizontal domains, imagining trends, sequences, portraying

systems, factors, formulations, identifying, and often I suppose ultimately concluding their work with a satisfyingly omnipotent flourish of naming. Of nomination. Of tagging with élan.

We have within organic taxonomy taxonomies, our kingdom, phylum, genus, species, all these categories for categorization. We never stop being victims

of our tendencies to generalize. We rarely forget how to compare.

There are 19 causal categories within four levels of human failure, so say the taxonomists of accident analysis who do their work in the everyday actuarial.

There are slips and lapses and mistakes enumerated.

There are routine violations in exceptional circumstances.

There are instances of extreme noncompliance.

There are quotidian errors.

We have identified over 700 individual accidents.

We have classified these.

We have charted, mapped, outlined, and made an art of diagrams.

There are those among us whose eyes find means to give us relationships among varieties,

who summarize and show us, in simple-to-read representations, ideas that become factual manifestations.

The front of me is always on one side of the moon or the other.
See how dark I can be, now, and how bright, some other times obliterated.

How romantic are the chemicals of which we are made

wax, salt, semen, water

he was an ancient Marxist baby

he ate anteaters with triceps

they were bicephalous and gusty

you could see what made him quiver

women really are more exciting, and they can't help
that, no one should hold it against them

what's to become of idle talk in public places

or when one realizes one talks too much and one
fears the results

of what talking too much can be, when one's made
to understand: everyone wishes you would say less
than you say

everyone wishes you would stop talking, everyone is
being polite pretending they are listening

why it is best of all to be an orphan

why all the most famous heroes are orphans, aban-
doned or otherwise lacking a family

a family can be a burden, such a complex burden,
such a bounty

we are frightening and obvious and melodramatic,
first we are babies, the most helpless humans on
earth

you wanted some Lucretius candy
didn't you

not that I believed in it but because it was expedient

not that it was true

it was thought to be true by other people at other
times and I listened

& that fact—I knew they believed in it—could not—
why should it—
be denied

The Usual Ratio of Banality to Wonder

When someone looks back longingly, maybe in
      wonder, back toward
their past and says, I don't have a father, my father
      disappeared when I was a little girl,

or someone says something like this, someone
      says, no I never knew my mother, she killed
herself in front of me

when I was five, it's true, I feel so bad (for who?
      the mother? the father? myself? you? us all?)
something direct and wordless happens in my
      chest. All my strongest

feelings happen in there where I can't help but
      understand them to be true.
So then when and if something I'm feeling gets
      outside of me, like this,

it can tend to seem superficial or shallow or
    insincere, or some of all
the ways there are over & across the suspect
    spectrum of emotions

we call meaningful & sincere, but suspect a little,
    we can't help but
suspect how they look, how they might look out
    there

on the outside, when exposed, sometimes
    someone says it's none of my business
to feel what others feel

but once I'm told something that matters
    monumentally, it's inevitable, I'm going to feel
this, if not in my heart, right up next to my heart
    where what happens on account of

anything someone's told me takes hold and
    changes who I am.
And starts up another feeling simultaneously, a
    strikingly obvious feeling

of being alive and human. Something that
   obvious and that taken for granted
most of the time, and dangerously close to
   sangfroid's calm or equanimity's nerve.

If anyone wants a poet usually they want their
   poets to be saying something,
if not for them, then at least apparently having
   them somehow or other in mind,

maybe to take up talking about something,
   whatever that might be, that matters to them.
To speak up for them. To not leave them out, or
   just hanging there.

People like love poems, and poems in which we
   talk to the dead
because talking to the dead is something everyone
   does at one time or another.

Someone will want to see how others talk to
   people who are no longer around.
Or they'll be looking for someone else to be
   filling in where they left off.

People like how a poem is one place (there are
    others) we believe talking to the dead
might have the results we desire and intend. In
    us, for others, beyond.

Some people like love poems because just about
    everyone's experienced how impossible it can
be to have words come out of your mouth when
    you're at first in love.

It's impossible. Being speechless is how that is
    and should be. When you're first in love you
shouldn't have so much to say. You should be
    communicating by other means.

And so poets take up the slack and write love
    poem after love poem after love poem,
I know I've done it. They're my favorite kind of
    poem to write.

I saw the phrase "the usual ratio of banality to
    wonder" and it arrested my attention for the
certainty it proposed. I thought immediately—
    really? Someone knows this?

People would like to hear poems about fear, every
    kind of fear that's common to being human.
Fear of being not good enough, or being left out
    in the cold, or shunned, or told

to go away, you don't belong here, or fear of being
    made to feel less than worthwhile, or fear of
being unloved or betrayed or of being one huge
    disappointment to anyone who

matters, or fear of getting sick or fear of dying or
    fear of never being loved. And then for some
people fear of fear is the subject they'd like to hear
    poets say something about.

People fear many things, during the turn of the
    20th century to the 21st fear has practically
been our national pastime, our collective hobby,
    our password, byword

into a land of paranoia so that often we're made
    to find our minds paralyzed or numbed,
or we're panic-frozen by traumas that will not go
    away. Everyone knows that fear

is the worst control. And the most effective. To
    lead someone to fear must be one of
the most unkind, most destructive things any one
    of us has ever done.

People want poems to say things about money and
    work and what it means to have more or less
of those, and what that does. People want to
    know what money means.

They want poets to say something about money
    even if it means the poet is going to have to be
embarrassed by it. Poets are required to endure
    any and all embarrassments.

Most poets say they don't like to talk about money
    but they're always talking about money; once
you say anything in words, in public, to strangers,
    there's money around.

You may want to ignore it, and you can
    sometimes, but money isn't going away, if by
money we include anything of value we trade and
    barter for what we need to live.

Embarrassed poets are pretty worthless to
    humanity. An embarrassed poet is okay for
some things but not many. Think of what poets
    feel obligated to include in their poems.

By definition in the land of poetry nothing is
    forbidden.
And that is in itself sometimes frightening, and
    something to be feared.

Sometimes people like to see a poet own up to
    something awful in a poem, and sometimes to
see a poet accuse someone, or sometimes all of
    humanity, of terrible things,

things so unspeakably wretched it's a wonder
    words stand being able to contain them,
some things people say ought to be taken to the
    grave & lo and behold, they too often are.

It's not a joke to believe that by means of poetry's
    metaphorical essence we're able to
understand a little better what to do with the
    complexities of which we're composed.

When Auden says *poetry makes nothing happen* he's
 praising how poetry takes anything and
everything and honors its existence by being its
 shadow, ghost, and soul.

Giving what's invisible a chance to be visible for at
 least a little time.
Or at least it's proposing what it might be like if
 what's essentially invisible

might be seen. Proposing a solution to
 omniscience's opposite, maybe to be seen.
It turns nothing into something, or what appears

to be nothing, into the many things it is. Poetry
 knows better than I do what to do
with regret, and shame, and disappointment and
 weakness of the will and spirit.

Unless one's brain finds cause to be well used,
 what happens in any poem
can feel useless or some kind of worse wasting of
 time. And if a poem seems

to want to hold you or anyone else hostage it turns
    itself into something suspect
and it begins to seem to want more from you than
    you from it, injustice prevails.

Poetry brings everything back for us (as do other
    things, our brain, our eyes, dance, keys,
water, air, space, light, skin and bones, terrain,
    birds, underwater creatures, ants, salt,

hooves, horns, strings, synchronized,
    harmonized, hands, hair, pouring, standing,
music, sleep, wind, seeds, dirt, shale (when a
    photographer says "I photographed

things because I wanted to see how they looked in
    photographs," the truth of
that is some kind of balm and comes home. Who
    would want to argue with that?)).

Tautology seems like nothing in art. And that's
    lucky, maybe for us all.
Poetry can stand to hear anyone scream. Within
    its borders, the idea of

borders never can be forever erased, to stand
    accused will be soul-destroyingly
worse than having this happen on any ordinary
    day in any everyday court of law.

People want poems about loss and how to grieve
    honorably and thoroughly.
They want poems that seem to keep the memory
    of someone alive

or at least give them the impression that how they
    feel about missing someone
is honorable and good for a human to do. They
    want poems to sentence.

And they want poems about dead horses and long-
    lost automobiles, and the kitchen chair
they kept for themselves for as long as their last
    lost love stayed alive.

As you can imagine there's no end to what people
    might want from a poem.
And what they might need. In a poem anyone can
    righteously accuse, collect evidence,

witness, hear testimony, argue, decry, submit,
    and build a case that without doubt
proves us all to be small, frightened, broken,
    valiant, bold, boring, and botched.

A poem will always be an unnecessary addition to
    what is always there, but a sign,
a signification that repeats itself for the sake of
    consoling us in our fleeting

consciousness and longing, always that, always
    next, more, after, toward.
A poem will do what ought to be unnecessary but
    isn't ever merely or just.

It exists unnaturally unless you count as natural
    everything humans make.
It's made by a mind's effort, a heart's will, out of
    the stubbornness we are.

And it is important for a poet to keep in mind
    other ratios, the ratio of responsibility to
carelessness, the ratio of love without end to
    patience without reward, the ratio of

innocence to violence, the ratio of foolishness to
    dignity, of reasoning to justification,
of strength to weakness, of self-preservation to
    greed, of willingness to destroy to

forgiveness, of what's rational to what's beyond
    reason, of darkness to light and
how that shifts and changes through a lifetime and
    through the hours of a day.

It's true that people like to be surprised by what
    they find in a poem, to find something
they hadn't anticipated finding there, & for this to
    be authentic it needs to be true

for the poet also, the poet's arrivals within the
    poem must, at least most of the time,
be authentically unintended. A reason formal
    shapes and conditions can be good

for making poems is because in them all of our
    human desires to be orderly and shapely and
clear and simple and repetitive and musical and
    word burned can be satisfied

so that the rest of the poem can go on unimpeded
    by what's predictable or predetermined
by what poets have heard before or what the
    newspapers happen to report in their reports

about recent scientific or psychological or
    political surveys and studies, investigations
based on one point of view's gathering of
    information, or creation of statistics or what

the poet remembers about her childhood or what
    the poet thinks you want to hear.
It takes little more than calling something a poem
    to both elevate what's within

whatever that is, and to diminish, sometimes
    pitilessly, sometimes vainly, sometimes
purposely on purpose to rouse or propose the
    question *what's a poem* to a status more

important, more significant than it is or would
    ever want to be. A terrible distraction.
Without this paradox we're left behind, we might
    as well avoid the light of day.

The Doorknob

FOR GUY

It could happen—

the one

the one & only one

or two

really important things,

the two

the two things

to explain it all

to explain everything

the doorknob

for instance

the one always creaking

sideways,

the dog

who always

looks sidewise

as if she never really

sees you the same

as you are

the same

the same window frame

inconsequential things

as things can seem

halfway registered

off to the side

things that get dropped, or ignored,

evaporated

or

disappeared

no longer here

by accident—

as if your life

had the permanence

of all matter put together

as if there were some way out

from where we are

and somewhere in

to what's not been—

a little bit of one sad story

because it will be the one story

the one and only story really

in which you fail to recognize yourself

as in

you'll be the hero and

you'll be the villain

and you'll be all the peripheral characters

whose purposes

for being there really only are

to decorate or populate

the place with other people

you'll be the hero

all right

but you won't be

who you thought you were

it's not easy to decide

what to leave out

what to ignore

what to say nothing about

what to call expendable

—and think about it—

think about all

you forget

or fail to register—

—you probably forget exactly what

you should have remembered

everyone that night

skirting around one another

circling around and

around both

wanting

to be near one another

wanting to be close

enough

wanting to be sure

every one is present

and accounted for

and at the same time

no one wanted to be so close

that feeling one another's temperature

would be only a matter

of paying a little bit closer attention

every one felt afraid for every one else

every one knew how damaged every one was

every one felt the damage

their own and every one else's

damage to spare

who was the hero—

which one took that role and stole

the show—

to say one of us knows

the whole story is just another suspect

story part

there's always some one

who thinks they know it all

because some one has to take that part

there's always one

who knows more than anyone else

and there's always one who

doesn't

want to know anything

that's hard, that's too hard to bear

the chronology of the story

takes its shape

from the bare-boned chronology every

one of us shares

one day or night or dawn or dusk you're born

you walk, you talk, you run,

you have more birthdays

you have more

you have several

you make friends

you fall in love

you go to school

you maybe marry

you maybe find

something to do with yourself

you like to do

to pass the time

and that coincidentally

brings in resources sufficient to

as they say, keep

your head above water

that turns out to be a luxury

just keeping one's

head above water

treading water where somewhere there is water

at least there is enough water to tread

water deep enough to tread in,

and there's access to it

that's not limited

by physical obstacles and

is okay for you to be in it

it isn't poisonous or off-limits

it's not the town's drinking water supply

there's no no

trespassing sign

surrounding it

or warning to keep away from it

because

it doesn't belong to you

and you have no right to that water

you have so many secrets

and so many secret lives

there's no cause to talk

about it as you assume

it's the case

with every one else

and just as the surface

already is beyond

understanding

and to add to this

this and all else

endlessly disturbs and turns & chills

A Style

when I think of him waiting for me to come to him
when then was now

when it was he who might have
as if how now moves around goes on

an understanding of what conditions
I would be barely able to bear

when now happened to be then
now more than ever

and how it takes feelings
to turn into convictions

and how indecision
breeds weakness

and how brutal weakness is
and what tolls it takes

a conviction
after many attempts

to forgive him
it became clear

there was nothing there to forgive
nothing for forgiving to lay its weak hand upon

a style of conviction in indifference
a conviction of style

a signal
like an army's uniform

a battalion of men on motorcycles escaping their
    pasts without destination
an identification like

a hairstyle
like a list of names

like saying a cup of water is unconvincing
or saying a man is an unconvincing person

the cold indifference of names carved in stone
dropped down a well

one of the few places sound goes to gain materiality
the well of a missile silo

maybe a well where the child fell in
and we saw you do it

Being Mortal Is There Mercy in It?

FOR EMILY

if music were on this page
music as music itself is

paradoxically making an appearance as if
without materiality

and rightfully in and of
its own particular wavelengths

not the music we talk about when we
go on

about the music there is
in words

when we talk about
that sound and

those acoustics
a word produces

depending on how
and who

says it and what for,
one thing when it's whispered

into a welcoming
and open ear

something altogether not like that
when it's not

welcome
there

and not welcome
at all

something like
when it's an altogether other

kind of sound
when it sheers

or shrieks or spins
out beyond itself

into audible physical battering
beating beyond

because before
besides because because

because
when it's screamed or hissed

or coldly chipped
like ice taking a break

before it breaks back
into water and

one way when
it's shaped

to suspend one's sense
another when

it's twisted
beyond belief

to skip sense over
and if there is music

on this page
as say in a layover

and over and under
the way music can

come and go
anywhere it pleases

so that this page
could not be still

or be the page it is
if music could

underwrite this page
if it could hold this page up

or wipe this page out
if it could stand

in stead of it
if all that it is

could go on about it
if it could all be otherwise

or if music could be all there is
left in the world

which sometimes it surely seems
it should

or could be so as in
when we get lost in music

which is the only way
music means to be

the one way we mean it when
we say we're lost in it

even that would
not be enough,

it would not be sufficient
to stop

the bleeding grief absence is
for

these words would
have such life

in and so of them
they would burn

in ways
so present

we would begin
to smell smoke and think *fire*

if on this page
there was the music you

brought to me
when you saw how music

was more than my lifeblood,
more than my soul,

with such life it
would burn beyond

this pitiful presence
I seem to be always leaving

being today of all days
what with there being

a limited number
from which to choose

of all days the day
in December

when we first arrived
on earth

finding one another once,
twice, many times over

just about around
every corner

just about
only for not neither

any other
just about nearly always

your presence arrives
and once arrived

how simple it all is
even if all it really is

is feeling compassion drift
into love

or sorrow drift into passion
or thankfulness drift

into love and beyond
love

to see into what exactly
maybe as if maybe

it might could be written
in The Saddest Story

in The Sorriest Words
in The Saddest Sentences

in the The Saddest Book
anyone is doomed to read

it isn't good to begin
to believe

how useless
it can be

to want more
than what one is given

or to see so far
into the distance

one can see
where one's headed

long before
one arrives there

with or without
music or the very idea

of music the way it is
the way any word has

to have a kind of music in it,
to hold within itself

or to contain what's heard
or never heard

with or without
being understood

to be essential and definitive
and maybe

what's beautiful about any
exponentially quintessential

multidimensional exploded
view of all there is

any and every where
or to have some

kind of music
anyway

as the near, at, the, very being
held in reserve

and then to let it go,
escape,

run away, fly, race toward,
& leave evidence of

its knowledge behind
to go where words are not

the words we know
so that materiality

appears as if it is just as certain
as spots (there's a trace left)

on a leopard
about to take down a baby gazelle

after having done with its mother,
if music were on this page

the way words' shadows are
any beloved's death

would not wreck us
in the same way

instead it would make some kind
of unkind sense

and you would be back
to where you were

if there were music on this page
the way music

hides or bursts forth
from every word

there is
supposing there has to be

at least one
and maybe even a handful

of people who realize
the inkling

of the situation
requires

a lack of awareness
of our inexpensive mortality

and all it bears
to bear the way

we know exactly
what it means

when we hear someone tell us
a hand-me-down story

about a house
with one window more

on the inside than on the outside,
here, we counted them,

remember how
it is to count something

so as to recognize its value,
ten died here, 10,000 there,

more on the outside
than on the inside

and what that means
and more on the inside

than on the outside
and what that means

as in let's pretend
there has to be just one

who opens her eyes,
looks around and sees

someone she loves go away
without end

with no means
to end it, no means to stop it

and not so much to put an end to it,
no one can stop that,

but to understand
a little better

and learn to live with
and thus live less in fear

Pathological Empathy

It irritates us
& what might that be

as in
it drives me crazy

something nearly nothing
& really irrelevant

something almost nothing
something from one's childhood

that changes you forever
so much so

it's unforgettable
like Fellini

the first time
or some song

I like how people like to think
of the end of the world

from time to time
how small we let ourselves be

to be able to say
beginning with everything beginning

to be never-ending
because we can imagine that

because our minds do that to us
without fail

drilling down paradox directly into us
as sure as sure can be

right from the beginning
and what is that anyway

something to be sad to lose
to be knowing

if not now eventually
something to be crying over

when anyone complains
how poems are hard to understand

for instance
aren't they really complaining

that life is impossible
to understand

and that we spend most of it
keeping ourselves distracted

from that unanswerable
and therefore, what,

idiotic line of questioning
as it turns out

most comparisons are,
as if

the love of one's life's death
can be compared

to the worst breakup of all time
or as if some of what

you miss
you never knew to miss it

or anyone who knows
the feeling of waiting

through the night
for a loved one to appear

and to be put away
for safekeeping

or how it is when
a fever subsides

or a cough is codeine quelled
or a fever breaks

and one no longer stands
on the edge of panic

I Didn't Know Before

What's a nemesis for
but to learn more

about right proportion
and to

become who knows who
can distribute one's fortune.

Your duty became my fate.
Or so someone said.

And you did.
You did distribute

my fortune
as if

you were

what made it rain.

When you

threw me

to the wolves,

my fortune, such as it is,

stays with the wolves,

where you

of all people know

is where I've always preferred

to be. Dear

distributor

of fortune,

of the future,

you are neither

good nor bad,

at least that's what they
like to say you are.

You always mean
to pass along

in due proportion
to each of us

according to what we deserve.
Any resentment caused by any disturbance

of this right proportion
it is your lot to distribute.

Any sense of justice
that cannot allow

injustice to pass
unpunished,

just resentment,
just balancer,

just balancer of fortune's chance,
punisher of hubris

from whom
there is no escape.

Punisher
of those who

disdain anyone who loves,
as they say,

indiscriminately,
punisher

of those
who have too much good in them,

cursed those
with gifts to spare

a jealous god, &
an envious one.

More monstrous,
how useless

to see
anyone grieve

to mourn and to mourn and to mourn
some more

to say it is sadness
you feel for

that one who is gone
but the truth may be

that once upon a death
who's dead and has died

transfers
to take on becoming

a symbol
a symbol of something

a symbol
symbolizing

unlike any other
on earth

otherwise
it wouldn't be so

misunderstood
it should not be

the only ones
who really know

when they're going to die
are the suicides

who leave us terrified
& never tell us

how it feels to know
why

(why can't they?)
do they forget

to tell us
being distracted

by what must be
one of the most unusual

typically unrepeatable
feelings on earth?

May be they don't
want to tell

us & that not
untypical thing

people say
about suicide

—that they were
really angry

but maybe they weren't angry
maybe they were busy

doing something else
doing something unlike

anything
else

maybe we like to think
they were angry so

that we can at least include ourselves
in the story

maybe even include ourselves
in the story's motive

maybe when we say someone is gone
we are saying how

they cannot linger nor any longer
be themselves

not now, not since
nor ever after

transitioning
into becoming

symbols
someone

can't be both someone
and a symbol

at the same time
as a symbol

someone's meaning becomes
narrowed

and limited
as a symbol

someone becomes static
and that static state

includes
being no longer

anyone at all
so that when we say

we miss someone
who's died

we are saying a true
and simple thing

we are saying
what is so

when we are
missing someone

who is no longer with us
we are saying what is true

Autophagy Irrespective

many times trees took a bullet
on our behalf, on the battlefield,

for what
the short time

I'd ever been inside a body,
relative to time,

as the way time is always
inside any body

can't be blamed
for failing to understand

its ins and outs,
what it needs

and what it might
need to avoid,

or beyond all get-out
how it sometimes reacts

it is still, it is rampant,
it is accurate, omnivorous,

you are something
to see

you come regaled
with what's already everywhere

on just about any day
when you see someone

who otherwise isn't a bad,
a terrible person (like me)

like what to write does
while it goes on

to anybody
taking a kind of pleasure from

finding someone else's pain
there's a name for that,

it has a name,
an alternative

is to explain
how it expands

the meaning
of taking pleasure

to include whatever
it is that can make a human senseless—

of the pain's invention
so readily provides,

one can be more
grateful to be alive

no matter the motive,
no sense for the others

fear of revenge
fear of guilt going

hand in hand,
hand in glove,

head in hand
—better to feel one will

be unfairly punished
for another's crime

than to look hard
into one's own very soul

for the stirring in there
of casual hatreds

thoughtless cruelty and crimes
hand in hand

with crimes
against humanity

not a single crime of passion
against one individual person,

a private motive of hatred
or revenge, greed or just getting ahead

as in a story
about members of a murderer's home

becoming more afraid
for their lives

as paths cross
with any place

we're in
we believe

we can never leave

is that so—little
do we remember

how easy it is
to leave one another

how we slip away
without fanfare, fuss, or bother,

moving away
as on a moving sidewalk

via
a revolving door

to face momentarily
a monumentally

false door
looking all too much

like a door opening
before dematerializing

and passing
through it,

through and through
one of those doors

before doors
in the antechambers

of our hearts' desires
in the pre-front-loaded areas

we stupidly presume
to get,

to get as if
we understand,

the vacuum doorways
in the safety chambers

the French doors,
the sliding doors,

both halves of half doors,
rotation

rotation in the revolving
doors

we are stuck in
you will not make a move

to get out of
a revolution of

white-white & off-white flowers
and the evil smell

of stargazer lilies before
let outdoors to breathe

so the air they absorb
isn't all the air there is

so at dusk
they can attract bats

all the same
as before as before as before

as you belong as you breathe
as you know along

with everyone else
how ridiculously we behave

when it falls to us
to reason to realize

how on our good days
the situation

we're born into
most likely ought not be questioned

how it is a gain
how without question it

remains
as far

as long
as these particular circumstances

stay
to multiply

exponentially
in addition to

adding more
meaning raining

down on us
down on us

from how far
from how far

from above
raining down on us tonight

Acknowledgments

Thanks to Wave Books for making this book possible;
David Caligiuri for reading with hawk eyes and to
Heidi Broadhead and Matthew Zapruder for bring-
ing it to life, thanks to Arda Collins, James Haug,
Lesle Lewis, and John Emil Vincent for reading it,
and with thanks to the editors who brought to light
earlier versions of some of these poems, *Conduit*,
Divine Magnet, *Epiphany*, *Granta*, *iO Poetry*, and *Rain Taxi*;
"The Usual Ratio of Banality to Wonder" was read
at *Rain Taxi*'s Anniversary Reading at the Walker Art
Center, Minneapolis, Minnesota in April 2015,
subsequently published as a poster-broadside by
Rain Taxi in April 2016.